Oscillographic Study Of The Singing Arc

John Ezra Hoyt

In the interest of creating a more extensive selection of rare historical book reprints, we have chosen to reproduce this title even though it may possibly have occasional imperfections such as missing and blurred pages, missing text, poor pictures, markings, dark backgrounds and other reproduction issues beyond our control. Because this work is culturally important, we have made it available as a part of our commitment to protecting, preserving and promoting the world's literature. Thank you for your understanding.

OSCILLOGRAPHIC STUDY OF THE SINGING ARC

THESIS

PRESENTED TO THE FACULTY OF THE GRADUATE SCHOOL OF THE
UNIVERSITY OF PENNSYLVANIA IN PARTIAL FULFILMENT OF
THE REQUIREMENTS FOR THE DEGREE OF
DOCTOR OF PHILOSOPHY

BY

J. E. HOYT (John Egree Hoyt)

PHILADELPHIA, PENNSYLVANIA
1911

OSCILLOGRAPHIC STUDY OF THE SINGING ARC.

By J. E. Hoyt.

THE line of work taken up by the author in this paper was suggested by the remark of the editor of the London Electrician (Vol. 46, p. 356) in reference to the Duddell arc. "One feature of this experiment was brought out in this paper, viz., there is an alternate current generated by the arc of the same periodicity as the note emitted, but the experiment failed to make this clear. We would like to know if a telephone receiver placed in the circuit of the arc would emit a note that might be analyzed into only the same elements as the tone set up in the arc itself, or whether there are current variations set up other than those to which the shunt causes the arc to resound. In other words if Mr. Duddell's musical instrument were introduced into a telephone circuit, would the receivers in the circuit play the same tune as the arc itself, or would a jangle of other sounds be superposed upon the tune? Another question, if two or more arcs in series were to be separately shunted for different tones, would a telephone in series with all the arcs emit the chord combining the several tones?" No reports of work done along that line have come under this author's observation. Therefore it occurred to him that a qualitative study of the wave forms and of the harmonics present in the oscillations, and their relationships to the various conditions of the shunt circuit, of the arc itself and of the inductance in the source circuit, would be of interest. It was planned to make an oscillographic study of the resultant effect of two or more parallel circuits shunted about the arc, each with its own capacity and inductance, recording the current in the shunt circuits and in the arc at the same time.

The arc that was used in these experiments was an ordinary hand feed, vertical arc, capable of various adjustments, one of the electrodes being water cooled. The water furnished an atmosphere of vapor and produced stronger and more constant oscillations. Unless otherwise specified the electrodes were solid carbons 6–8 mm. in diameter. In the source circuit was usually connected as chokecoil, the primary of a transformer, and also a bank of incandescent lamps in parallel. The oscillograph was one of the G. E. type, having three bi-filar suspension systems. These were calibrated so that volts or amperes could be read directly from the curves. For the inductance of the shunt circuit there were two coils of

300 turns each of No. 10 wire, wound on cylinders 30.3 cm. in diameter and 93 cm. in length. The total resistance of one of these coils was about .9 ohm. The inductance was computed from Russell's formula,

$$L = (\pi dn)^2 l \left[1 - 0.424\left(\frac{d}{l}\right) + 0.125\left(\frac{d}{l}\right)^2 - 0.0156\left(\frac{d}{l}\right)^4\right],$$

and was found to be 6.82 (10)^6 cm. Connection could be made at various points so that the total induction of the coil could be varied by steps of 2.27 (10)^6 cm., and a bare wire coil could be connected in for finer adjustment. Three standard boxes of 10 mf. capacity each were used. Thus the lowest frequency calculated from Duddell's formula (which gives approximate values for low frequencies) would be 330 oscillations per second. For oscillographic study of course a low frequency was necessary. A preliminary investigation of the reliability of the stroboscopic and acoustic methods of determining the frequency of the electric oscillations was first decided upon. For the former a Duddell falling plate oscillograph was called into service using the singing arc itself as source of light. After overcoming very many difficulties a record was obtained which unfortunately is too faint for satisfactory reproduction. However, as might be expected, the spots of light evidently appear most distinct just after the minimum point of the potential difference curve, which corresponds to the instant after the maximum of the current. It is very evident, as was expected, that the variation in light intensity and current are isochronous.

In order to compare the electric and sound vibrations, it was decided to construct a sound oscillograph. This apparatus, as finally set up, consists of the following: Mounted on a heavy horizontal frame, attached to a heavy stand, is a heavy brass elbow, holding a brass frame about four inches in diameter, which in turn holds a fine specially prepared parchment diaphragm. The latter frame is so constructed that the tension of the diaphragm can be increased to the point of rupture. A high tension was used in this experiment. Also rigidly attached to the horizontal frame is a block, bearing on its face a flat section of a thick-walled brass cylinder. In this cylinder vertically opposite each other are two screws, in the ends of which jewel bearings are set, and between them is mounted the needle bearing the mirror. For this needle, the smallest that could be found anywhere was taken, cut in two and the blunt end sharpened. The mirror is about .03″ × .1″. The horizontal "suspension" is of unspun silk attached to the diaphragm at one end, passing around the needle, and attached at the other end to a very light spring, piece of spring brass, or even a very light rubber fiber. In order to rotate the needle for adjustment of the mirror without changing the tension, the brass frame holding the needle was mounted on a brass platform. Two strips of spring steel held the frame against the block. Then by means of a screw at one side of the frame and a piece of spring steel at the other, the frame could be moved back and forth along the platform thus causing the fiber to rotate the needle without changing the tension. Two screws from the back of the block made it possible to tilt the frame, needle and mirror backward or forward as needed. Since the heat of the arc was much too great to bring near the diaphragm, it was necessary to make use of a parabolic reflector and parabolic megaphone to obtain sufficient energy at the diaphragm. However the acoustic apparatus responds to almost any noise in the room, and vibrates freely in response to the human voice or to a mounted tuning fork across the room.

In order to obtain simultaneous records a G. E. oscillograph was installed and a pencil of light from the third prism was intercepted with a right prism directing it through a hole in the side of the box, upon the acoustic system outside. From this mirror it was reflected back and onto the photographic film. The whole apparatus was connected up as in Fig. 1. The diagram of apparatus shows: *A.S.*, the arc source; *R.P.*, right prisms; *E.S.*, the electric oscillograph system; *A.O.S.*, the acoustic system; *P.M.*, the parabolic megaphone; *S.A.*, the singing arc; *P.R.*, the parabolic reflector. The connections for the singing arc show *S.A.*, the singing arc; *C.C.*, the choke coil; *S.R.*, series resistance in source circuit; *O*, the oscillograph loop; L_1, C_1 and O_1 represent the inductance, capacity and oscillograph loop for shunt number one; L_2, C_2 and O_2 have corresponding significance for shunt number two.

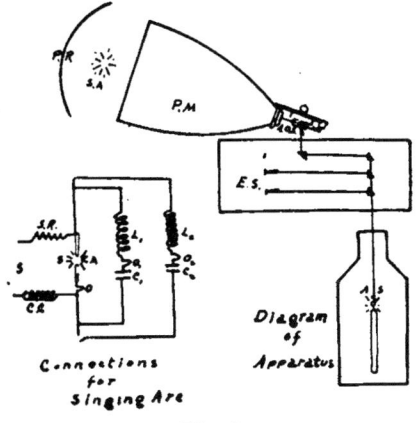

Fig. 1.

It was exceedingly difficult to obtain good records of the sound of the singing arc, for even while the arc is apparently constant as far as the ear could detect, yet the sound might be varying slightly in frequency. Even if the fundamental was constant, the harmonies due to conditions in the arc were changing in relative intensities and thus changing the character of the wave form. Still some very interesting records were obtained, probably the first acoustic records of the singing arc, surely the first obtained simultaneously with the electric records.

Several preliminary records were made of the harmonic vibrations of several tuning forks, vibrating simultaneously. These records suggested a use to which the acoustic system may be devoted,—the obtaining of accurate time values for electric oscillations of low frequency. For example simultaneous records were made of the variation of the arc potential and the sound vibration of Sol_3 fork. Comparing the two it was found that the frequency of the arc was about 420 os./sec. Computation by the simple formula

$$n = \frac{1}{2\pi}\sqrt{\frac{1}{Lc}}$$

gave a value of approximately 430 os./sec. From this it would appear that the simple formula will do for rough approximations in the case of low frequencies, especially where the resistance is very small compared with the other quantities involved.

Fig. 2 is a record of the acoustic oscillations of the arc, the current through the arc and the current in the oscillating shunt. It is very evident that the fundamental of the sound has the frequency of both the arc and the shunt circuit. The latter is reversed in direction, but can be seen to be very nearly the complement of the variation in the arc current, although the current through the arc appears to be more nearly a sine function. A single harmonic appears in the sound vibration, which does not appear in the current curve. This is probably due to mechanical effects of the impact of discharge rather than the electrical conditions. The capacity and inductance of the shunt circuit were 10 mf. and $6.82(10)^8$ cm. respectively, giving an approximate frequency of 600. The maximum value of the current is a little over 3 amperes.

Some approximate measurements were taken of curves representing the variation of current through the arc and also the variation of sound.

Time in Sec.	Arc Current in Amp.	Relative Values from Sound Curve.
0.	−2.6	−32.
$1.6(10)^{-4}$	+3.0	−15.
$6.4(10)^{-4}$	+0.2	33.
$9.6(10)^{-4}$	−2.0	+ 5.
$14\ (10)^{-4}$	−3.1	−10.
$15\ (10)^{-4}$	−3.0	0.
$18\ (10)^{-4}$	−2.2	−10.
$22\ (10)^{-4}$	+2.2	−31.

Fig. 3 represents the arc potential, current in shunt and acoustic vibrations for two shunt circuits, natural frequencies, 210 and 420. The value of the inductance in the smaller shunt is half that in the larger, as well as the value of the capacity. The maximum value of the current which is here the combined current of the two shunts is about 5 amperes, the variation in potential difference about 72 volts. The harmonic in the latter is very pronounced here though the sound was that of the lower frequency, so far as the ear could distinguish; the record, however, evidently shows at least one harmonic present. The fundamental evidently is in phase with the current through the arc, opposite to that of the shunt, but, though the current through this shunt is far from a simple wave form it is impossible to ascribe the harmonics of the sound to variations in the current. Here the current was oscillating quite freely in both shunts but when the arc is responding to the higher frequency the lower frequency shunt is unaffected and the current in the combined shunt —the arc—approximates more nearly the sine form. Figs. 4 and 5 show curves for same quantities under different conditions. In cases where the natural frequencies of the shunts were related as 2-1, the arc was liable to see-saw up and down, now giving the higher tone, now the lower, but in general the higher tone was more stable at smaller distances between the carbons, while the lower tone was more stable with greater separations. Especially was this true where the relationship was not a simple one. The higher tone was obtained most clearly and was most stable when the separation of the arcs was only .04 inch, but the lower tone was most stable with a separation of .1 inch or more. This would seem to indicate a sort of tuning or resonance effect. It will be noticed in regard to

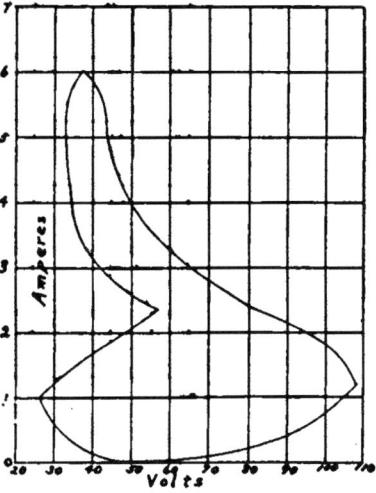

Fig. 6.
Dynamic characteristics. Pd. vs. current through arc.

the sound oscillations that the smoother and more sinuous the current curve, discharging through the arc, the simpler the sound oscillation. This might be explained on the idea of difference of impact in the arc.

Curves were also taken, showing the pd., current, and sound of arc, with no large inductance in the source circuit,—that is, with the choke coil removed. Two successive sets of curves were taken under the same conditions, only in the second, the coil was again inserted but the two sets are almost identically alike in form. Blondel has noted a difference in the quality of the tone under these differing conditions, but as far as the acoustic record goes there is no considerable difference in wave form though there may have been some difference in period. Each was recorded with the first harmonic, only.

Fig. 6 is a curve showing the dynamic characteristics of the singing arc. This was obtained by projecting simultaneous curves of pd. and current and tracing on a screen. Simultaneous values were then obtained and

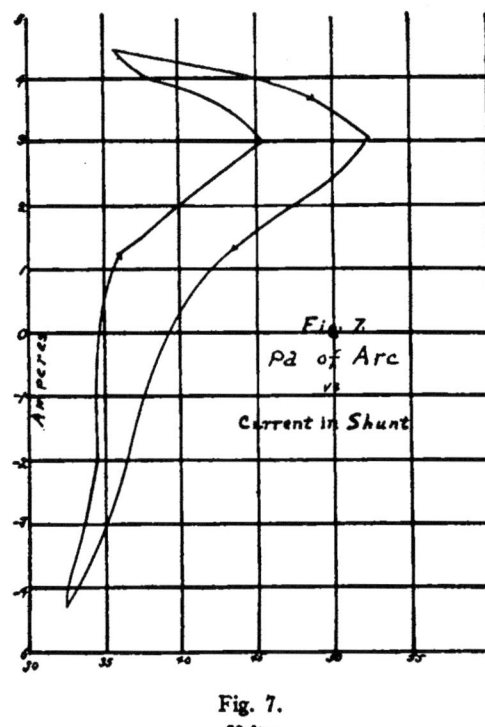

Fig. 7.
Volts.

plotted. It can be seen that the current of the arc actually reaches 0 in this case. Then with slowly rising current the potential rises rapidly, reaching a maximum, then the current rises more rapidly as the potential falls. For a brief decrease of potential, the current falls rapidly, then the potential starts to increase to a second maximum, decrease, then increase until the current reaches 0, when the cycle repeats itself. Thus for the greater part of the curve the dv/di is negative.

Fig. 7 represents the change of potential with variation of current in oscillating shunt. This, however, was with different constants in the oscillating circuit, about $5.12(10)^8$ cm. inductance and 30 mf. capacity. It will be noticed that with increasing current and decreasing inverse discharge we have a slight increase of potential for a time, then a more rapid increase, then a rapid decrease of potential with increasing current. With decreasing current the potential increases to a second maximum, then decreases rapidly to a minimum value with maximum discharge of condensers through the arc.

Fig. 8 shows the currents through the arc, and through each of two parallel oscillating circuits. The circuits were arranged to give relative frequencies of 2/1, when the arc responded to them separately, but they

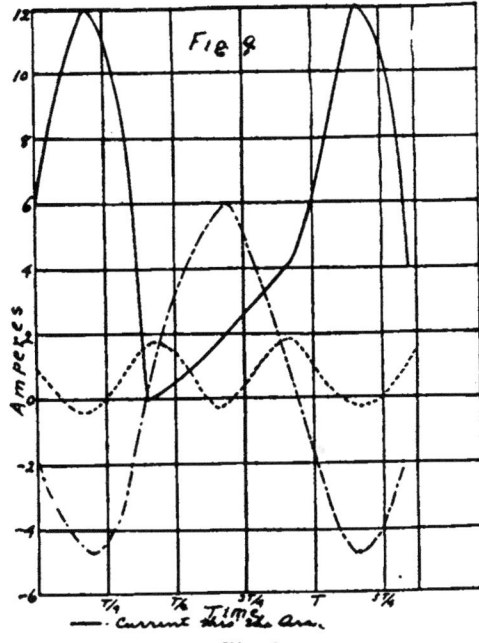

Fig. 9.

Solid line shows current through the arc; dotted line shows current through oscillatory shunt No. 1; broken line shows current through shunt No. 2.

simply produce a resultant effect regardless of the relative frequencies, generally oscillating with frequencies an octave apart. The discharge through the arc is far from a sine function, and the discharge through the oscillating circuit appears much more nearly a sine wave. Fig. 9 shows the relative values of these quantities; *i. e.*, currents in arc and shunt circuits, on a larger scale, drawn from a projection of a negative, on a screen. Apparently from this, the currents in the oscillating shunts are not quite sine functions, though more nearly so than the current through the arc. Apparently the current in the arc should equal the sum of a constant d.c. and the sum of the discharges due to the shunt circuits. The current through the arc when not oscillating was about 7 amperes. The maximum value of the current in the arc is very nearly equal to the sum of the inverse discharges and this value. But in the neighborhood of its minimum value this does not hold true. Evidently the wave form would be affected by temperature of the carbons, ionization and inductance of the arc. The current is seen to rise very gradually at first then more suddenly as might be expected.

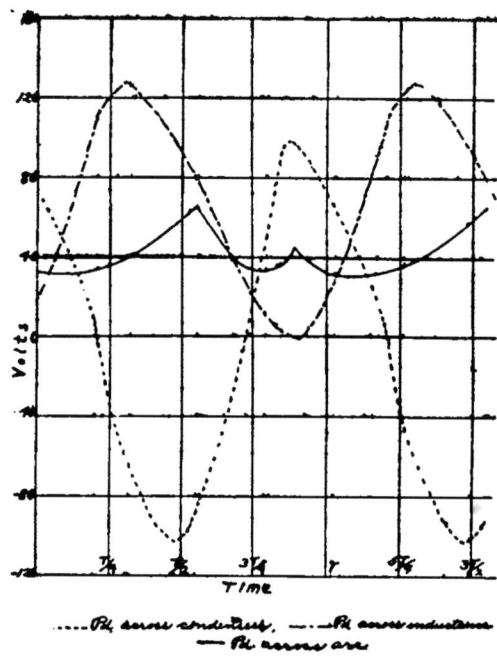

Fig. 11.

It was desired to find the relationship between the arc potential and the variation of potential differences at the terminals of the condenser and the coil in the single oscillating shunt. This is shown in Fig. 10. Fig. 11 shows a similar curve to a larger scale. The great variation in the pds. of the parts of the shunt contrast with that of the arc, the pd. variations of which bear little resemblance in amount or in phase with the individual variations or the vector sum of the pds. of condenser and inductance. It is quite evident that there must be something in the arc itself which influences the variation of potential, more than the conditions of the oscillating circuit. In general when the resulting potential of the shunt was rising the arc potential was falling and vice versa.

Fig. 12 shows the variations of potential across the arc, and across the condensers of the two oscillating circuits when the shunt circuits are tuned to the octave. Fig. 13 shows the same conditions as are represented

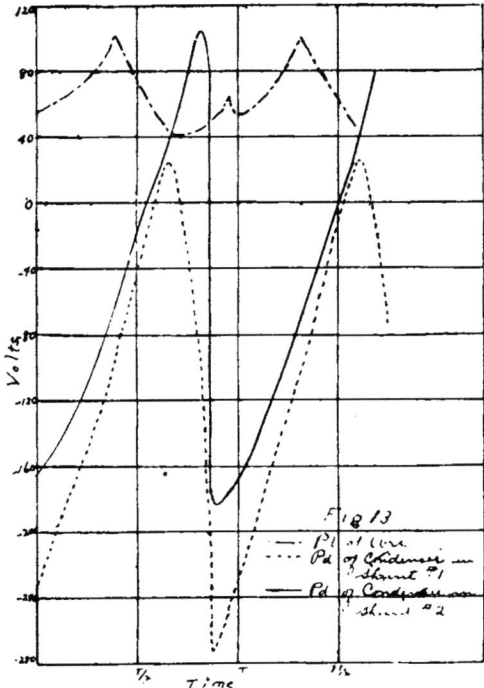

Fig. 13.

in Fig. 12, on a larger scale. The effect of adding another shunt was to produce a further relative phase shift. Furthermore the zero of these shunt curves is not the potential of the negative carbon, but about − 45 volts and − 120 volts respectively. It will be noticed through what a wide range the oscillations pass. The time of maximum current was not the same for each circuit and the rate of discharge was different, but the time for complete reverse discharge was about the same.

SUMMARY.

Oscillograph curves are here reproduced from photographs, of varied electrical conditions of the singing arc. In the case of a single shunt the current in the arc is very nearly a sine curve and its frequency can be approximately determined from the simpler Duddell formula. The current through the arc is approximately that of the oscillating circuit superimposed upon the d.c. The effect of adding a second shunt is to cause the arc current to deviate largely from the sine form, nor does it vary as the sum of the shunt inverse discharges. The current is evidently considerably affected by varying conditions in the arc. The arc potential does not even approximately follow the variation of the sum of the pds. of the condenser and inductance. The effect of introducing another shunt is to produce a phase shift in the condenser pds. which may have the same frequency of discharge even if of different natural frequencies.

An acoustic oscillograph was also constructed and herewith are reproduced the first acoustic curves taken of the singing arc, and possibly the first reproductions of simultaneous electrical and acoustic oscillations. Ordinarily for a single shunt it is found that the sound, which is isochronous with the electrical oscillations, is of a rather simple form, the oscillograms showing only a single harmonic. In the case where the arc current is more complex, as when two shunts are used, the resulting sound curve is quite complex. In the latter case the arc responds to one or the other of the shunt circuit frequencies, depending, $e. g.$, on the separation of the carbons. There seems therefore to be a sort of tuning effect, regulated by some electrical changes produced by opening or closing more or less the arc gap. This might possibly be explained by attributing the effect to the presence of induction in the arc, increasing with the separation. This inductive effect might also furnish the basis for an electrical explanation of the change of frequency with arc length which would be quite marked for higher frequencies where the inductance of the shunt is quite small. It is generally accepted that the singing arc discharge is rotational and that the pressure conditions in the arc are very peculiar.

No fundamental difference is recorded in the character of the sound oscillations for the two kinds of tones attributed to the oscillating discharge with and without inductance in the source circuit.

Considerable difficulty was early experienced in making the parts of the apparatus work together. Mechanical vibrations due either to the falling plate or the interaction of the motor and the oscillograph box to which the drum was attached, were hard to eliminate. The author is now designing an improved combined apparatus for the simultaneous recording of sound and electrical oscillations which he hopes to use for telephonic work, testing of diaphragms, etc.

In concluding, the thanks of the author are extended for the courtesy and suggestions of Professors Goodspeed and Richards, also for skilled assistance of Messrs. Jacob Martin and Kalmbach, in the construction of some of the apparatus.

RANDAL MORGAN LABORATORY,
   UNIVERSITY OF PENNSYLVANIA.
      June, 1911.

PHYSICAL REVIEW, XXXV
November, 1912

PLATE VI
To face page 396

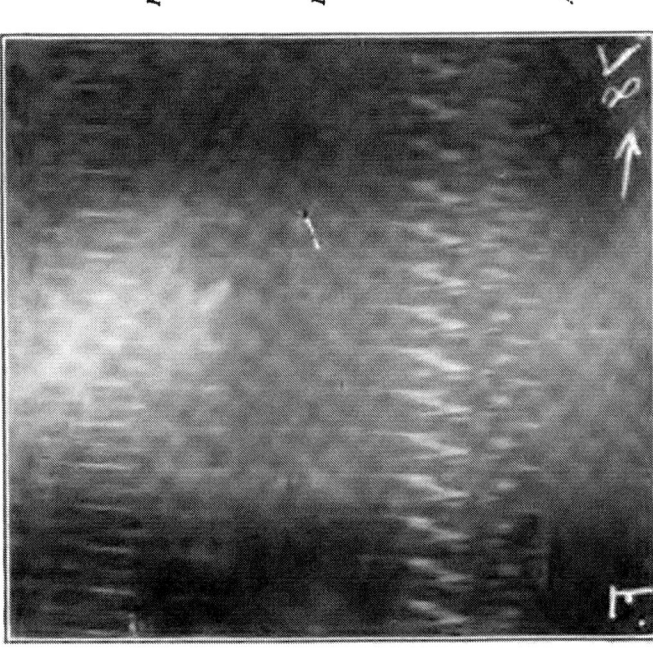

Fig. 3.

E = pd. of arc; I_1 = shunt current; A = sound vibration;
C_1 = 10 mf.; L_1 = 341 $(10)^4$ cm.; C_2 = 20 mf.; L_2 = 682 $(10)^4$ cm.

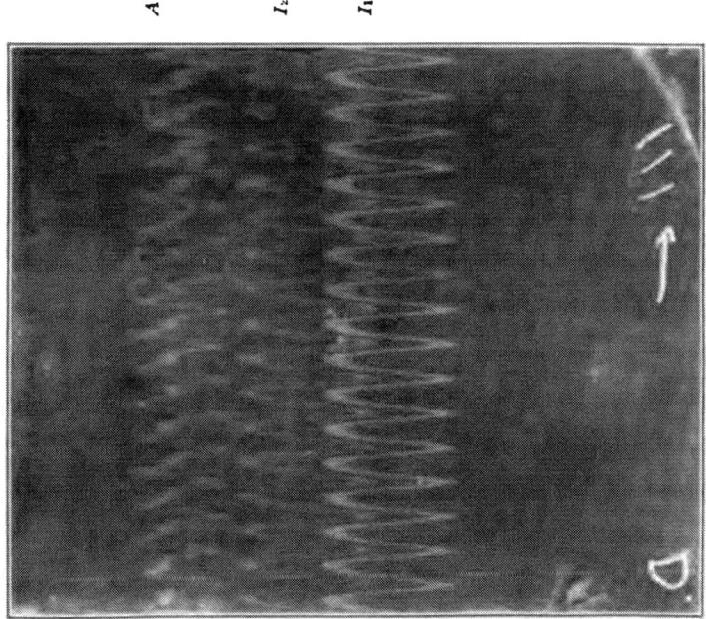

Fig. 2.

I_1 = current in shunt circuit; I_2 = current in arc circuit; A = mf.; L = 682 $(10)^4$ cm. acoustic oscillation; C = 10

J. E. HOYT

M to U

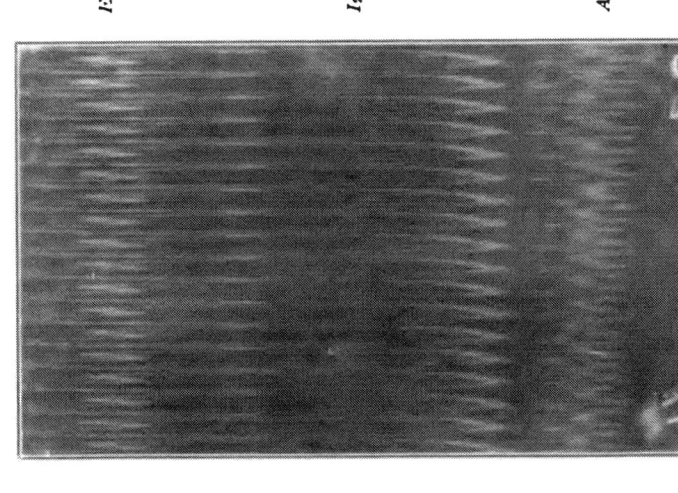

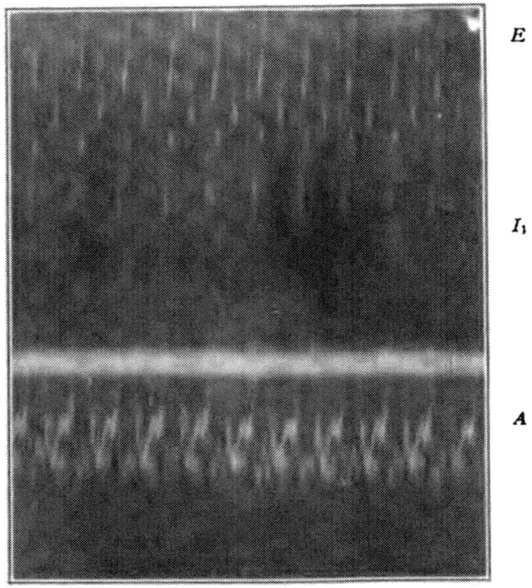

Fig. 5.
$C_1 = 20$ mf.; $L_1 = 682 \, (10)^4$ cm.; $C_2 = 5$ mf.; $L_2 = 682 \, (10)^4$ cm.

Fig. 4.
$L_1 = 682 \, (10)^4$ cm.; $C_1 = 10$ mf.; $L_2 = 170 + (10)^4$ cm.; $C_2 = 10$ mf.

MtoU

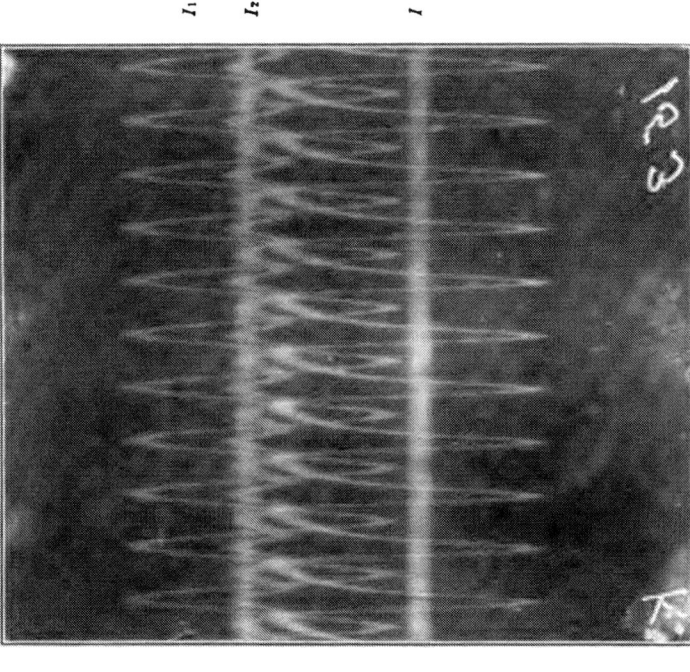

Fig. 8.

I = arc current; I_1 and I_2 = shunt currents; C_1 = 30 mf.; L_1 = 682 $(10)^4$ cm.;
C_2 = 10 mf.; L_2 = 341 $(10)^4$ cm.

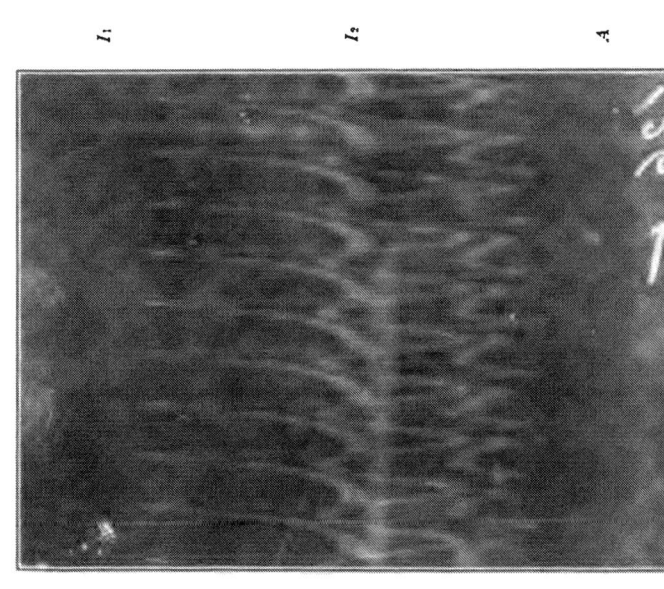

Fig. 5.4.

I_1 = current in arc; I_2 = current in shunt; A = acoustic oscillation;
C_1 = 14 mf.; L_1 = 682 $(10)^4$ cm.; C_2 = 14 mf.; L_2 = 170 + $(10)^4$ cm.

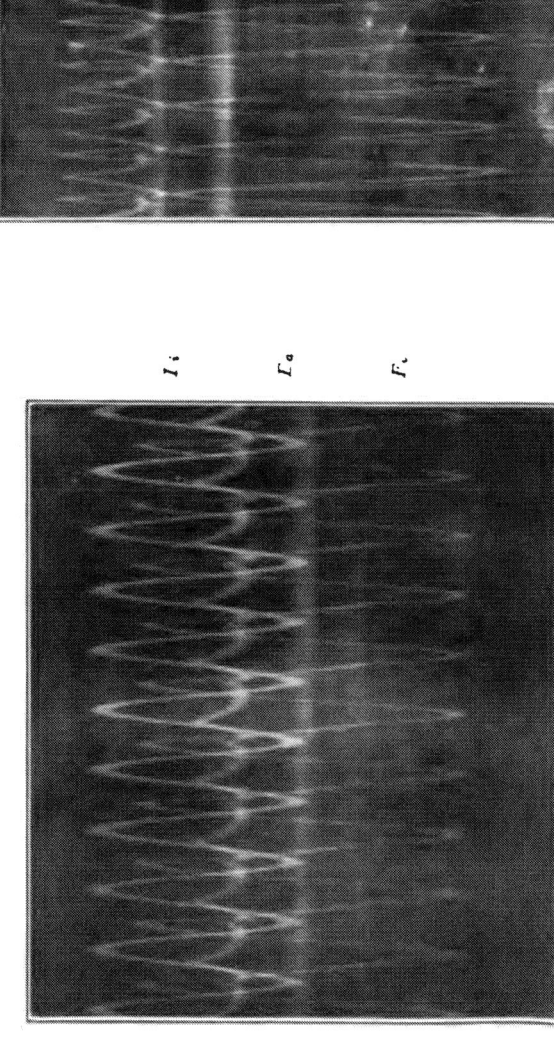

Fig. 10.

E_a = pd. of arc; E_c = pd. condenser; E_i = pd. of coil; C = 20 mf.; L = 682 (10)⁴ cm.

Fig. 12.

E_1, E_2 = pd.? shunt condensers; E_a = pd. of arc; C_1 = 8 mf.; L_1 = 6 82 (10)⁴ cm.; C_2 = 18 mf.; L_2 = .682 (10)⁴ cm.

Printed by Libri Plureos GmbH in Hamburg, Germany